MOTORING AROUND

SURREY

It is interesting to note the differences in dress and cars throughout the book: Left: Alfred Harmsworth, outside Sutton Place, Guildford, needs a full length fur coat to drive his 1902 Mercedes, which has neither a windscreen nor other weather protection.

MOTORING AROUND
SURREY

Bryan Goodman

TEMPUS

First published 2001
Copyright © Bryan Goodman, 2001

Tempus Publishing Limited
The Mill, Brimscombe Port,
Stroud, Gloucestershire, GL5 2QG

ISBN 0 7524 2360 6

Typesetting and origination by
Tempus Publishing Limited
Printed in Great Britain by
Midway Colour Print, Wiltshire

The Author and his 1900 BENZ P-275, outside a Reigate hostelry.

Contents

Nearly forty years after the picture on page two, this lady about to drive her 1939 Hillman, perhaps to a wedding, needs no special motoring clothing.

Introduction

Although I remember the last car my father had before the War and his first car after he came home again, my own interest in the story of the motor car was not kindled until I came home from National Service and bought my first car. It was a dreadful thing and quickly changed, on the advice of a friend, for something much older and it was then that my interest was born. That car is now the most modern of my old cars, and veteran and vintage cars have remained my hobby for nearly fifty years.

I have assembled here a collection of nostalgic photographs of cars – plus a few other vehicles to set the scene – all of which were taken in Surrey. Many cars in the county were registered elsewhere, either if the owner had another address, or because the car was registered by the supplier. It was also possible to register with a different authority to get specific letters, an example is Dennis Brothers of Guildford who used Stockport Borough Council to get the letters DB.

Many of the pictures are from my own collection but many friends and institutions who have allowed me to reproduce pictures are credited on page 128. There are inevitably photographers of many years ago that I cannot thank but would have liked to.

The motor car evolved over many years and through various stages of development. It did not appear fully formed and working in a particular year and yet it is essentially a modern phenomenon. Various people had created self-propelled vehicles throughout the nineteenth century but British invention was throttled by the 1865 Locomotives on Highways Act which required, amongst other things, that any self-propelled vehicle be controlled by at least two men with a third being required to go ahead on foot. At first the presence of two men on the carriage was not silly. The one at the back had charge of the boiler (hence the word 'chauffeur'), the engine and all the starting and stopping. The man at the front could only steer and pray! The man on foot was necessary to hold the heads of horses while the vehicle passed or to lead the horses past the stationary vehicle. Transport being limited to the speed and range of a pedestrian there was little point in building a car. Self-propelled vehicles were thus limited to traction engines, often towing a threshing machine and other trailers so the need for a man to help with harness-horses not used to such sights was necessary to ensure that those encountered did not bolt with their owners clinging to their seats.

Emancipation of the motor car followed the repeal of the Act in 1896. The 'Motor Car Club' decided to hold an event to demonstrate to the public that this new form of transport could be a practical proposition . Its members decided to drive from London to Brighton IN ONE DAY! That day was Saturday 14 November 1896 and of course some of the run was through the county of Surrey. It is this emancipation of the motor car that is still celebrated by the London to Brighton Run every November.

The Autocarists, as they were called, thought that a return on Sunday could bring bad publicity from a church-going population and the return for most of them was on the Tuesday. Car ownership only gradually gained favour and it is sobering to think that five years later (now one hundred years ago) there might have been less cars in the whole county of Surrey than are today parked in a single public car park of a single Surrey town.

In 1903 the Government saw the cash cow coming – though, to be fair, there were now sufficient cars about for licencing to be introduced too. By 1 January 1904 every private car owner had to purchase a licence, register the car with the county or county borough council, get a driving licence for themselves and their chauffeur and obtain and affix the numbers. All of which cost £4 15s 0d, which was quite an expense, and still left them to purchase and fit a tail-lamp to light that rear number.

Number plates began to appear at the end of 1903 ready for the first of January 1904. Each registration authority was allotted a single or double letter index mark. The letter for Surrey was 'P' but, within the old county of Surrey, Croydon was a County Borough and it was allotted 'BY'. Surrey's 'P' was used up (to 'P.9999') at the end of 1913 when the letters became 'PA' as follows:-

P 12/03 - 1913 PD 7/23 PK 5/28
PA from 11/13 PE 2/25 PG 5/29
PB 8/19 PF 3/26 PL 5/30
PC 7/21 PH 5/27 PJ 8/31

Three-letter indices were issued from October 1932 with the new letter added in front. Thus it started with APA, APB etc. but like the two-letter indices conversance with the alphabet was seemingly not part of the authority's mandate.

Croydon's 'BY' lasted until 1922 and then it was 'RK' from December 1922, 'VB' from June 1927 and 'OY' from January 1931. 'ABY' came in September 1934 and the sequence then follows with alphabetic tidiness which does not follow the two-letter order.

In many countries registration plates are the taxation receipt, as in the US, or issued to the owner rather than the car, as in Belgium and Switzerland. In France the last two numerals are those of the owner's department of residence, so a house move or sale of a car will often involve re-registration.

The British system is at least kind to the historian in that registrations issued remain with a car for its life and, however old, remain valid today. Less kind is the fact that neither Surrey County Council nor Croydon Borough Council retain any registration records before 1929.

Most car manufacturers of Surrey were ephemeral but there are honourable exceptions of course. Of the better known are:-

ABC Motors – Hersham
AC Cars – Thames Ditton
Allard in Putney until 1945
Dennis – Guildford
Frazer-Nash – Kingston
H.R.G. – Tolworth
Invicta Cars – Cobham until 1933 (and Virginia Water from 1946)
Lagonda – Egham, Staines
Railton – Cobham
Trojan – Croydon

And some of the others include:-

Beacon, Hindhead and Liphook (mentioned in this book)
Bleriot-Whippet, Addlestone
British Salmson, Raynes Park
Eric-Longden, Addlestone
Godfrey-Proctor, Richmond
Horley, Horley (also mentioned)
Marlborough-Thomas, Weybridge
Pilgrim, Farnham (also mentioned)
Tamplin, Cheam, from 1923
Warren-Lambert, Richmond, from 1919

This book is intended for the enjoyment of both the reader and author, rather than extensive education. I hope that some useful information will be gleaned alongside that enjoyment, and it will help build a picture of how the motor car fitted and affected Surrey lives in the first half of the twentieth century.

The book had to stop somewhere and I have chosen 1939. Both World Wars had an enormous effect on the history of private transport. In 1914 comparatively few people could drive or had any mechanical knowledge, but by 1918 the picture was different; many men had learned to drive during the war and were determined to spend their demobilisation grants on the purchase of a car, prompting some dreadful contrivances to be rushed onto the market. Within ten years the depression had truly set in, and very many companies failed to come through. These were both from the top end of the spectrum, like Bentley, and the popular market like Bean, Swift, Calthorpe and Clyno.

Bryan Goodman
November 2001

One
The 1896 Brighton Run
to the First World War

A cartoon from the *Illustrated London News* of 17 November 1906, ten years after the abolition of the Red Flag Act, shows the first small Benz car in England, Mr H. Hewetson's Benz of 1895. He was not allowed to use it unless preceded by a man with a red flag.

Hewetson was determined to advance the introduction of the motor car. When he first went out at Catford the local police were friendly but had orders from Scotland Yard to stop the car. The owner sent a bicycle scout ahead to report any policeman. Then a little boy, carried in the car, got down and carried a flag. The flag was only a tiny scrap of red ribbon on a pencil but it fulfilled the law.

Henry Hewetson began an agency for Benz cars in 1895 and the compiler's Benz of 1900 still carries Mr Hewetson's transfer.

FARNHAM'S HOSPITAL EFFORT

Full Description of the first two-seater Motor-Car made in England

THIS Motor-Car was made at the Reliance Engineering Works, West Street, Farnham, under the direction of and for the late J. H. Knight, Esq., by Geo. Parfitt, then foreman for the late G. Elliott and now one of the Proprietors of these Works. The car was started about February, 1895, this being 34 years ago, and on May 12, 1896, it was run at the Horseless Carriage Show which was held at the Crystal Palace in that year. There were also three other cars at the Show which were of foreign make, and this little car put up a good show there, and was on show at the Palace for some weeks. It was then returned to the above Works to have two front wheels fitted in place of the one front wheel, as shown in the above illustration ; it was then handed over to Mr. J. H. Knight and used by him. Mr. Knight came into contact with the police purposely for being on the common road without a red flag. This case was brought forward by a committee of gentlemen (J. H. Knight being one of them), and the law was then made for cars to run on our roads without the red flag. The car as you see it now has been in the private museum of Sir David Soloman, Bt., and the writer had not seen the car for 32 years before April 29, 1929. The car is now lent to help the above "Hospital Effort," and will be seen in the Carnival Procession by kind permission of Mrs. J. H. Knight, of Weybourne House, Farnham. There are now four other workmen beside Mr. G. Parfitt still at the Reliance Works who were there when the car was made. The writer thought the public would appreciate these few particulars and description of the said car, and in making a small charge of 3d. per copy it will be helping the "Hospital Effort" considerably.

(Signed) G. PARFITT.

Extract from an appeal for Farnham Hospital in 1929. Although the car has always been known as a Knight, it was largely constructed by the writer of the letter, George Parfitt. The car was much modified in the first few years of its life but by 1900 was quite obsolete. The John Henry Knight car still exists in its final form and is on display at the National Motor Museum at Beaulieu. Mr Knight lived at Barfield, Farnham.

This is where this book really starts, when motoring began in England. Until November 1896 it had been necessary to have two men on a "road locomotive" to control it and a third man had to walk in front, usually carrying a red flag. With speed thus limited it was really only traction engines that used the roads. They needed two men on board and with carriage horses not used to such sights the man on foot was necessary too to help hold the horses' heads.

There was a 'Motor Car Club' in 1896, ready to take advantage of the approaching freedom to use the roads and the repeal of the Locomotives on Highways Act was celebrated by a run from London to Brighton 'in one day' on Saturday 14 November 1896.

Shown above are three Panhard et Levassor cars stopping for lunch at the White Hart in Reigate on their way back to London on the Tuesday after the Run.

The front car was the winner of the Paris-Bordeaux-Paris Race in 1895 and was used as the 'Pilot-Car' on the London to Brighton Run, driven by Otto Mayer. The second car had been second in the Paris-Marseilles-Paris Race in September 1896, which readers of *The Autocar* were invited to go to Paris to witness. The charge for the trip by train from Holborn Viaduct or Victoria (second class), boat Dover to Calais, hotel in Paris, courier and guidebook and return to London was £5, leaving on a Wednesday and returning the following Monday. It was driven in that race and again here by Merkel. It probably has the Earl of Winchilsea as passenger. The third is a Harrods' van driven by E. Hankinson.

Over thirty years later, a veteran Daimler car passes the same hotel in the Brighton Run 1928. Since the Second World War the route has been along the A23, through Redhill.

THE AUTOCAR.

EDITORIAL OFFICES

19, HERTFORD STREET, COVENTRY.

PUBLISHING OFFICES

3, ST. BRIDE STREET, LUDGATE CIRCUS, LONDON, E.C.

A RED-LETTER DAY.

To-day, November 14th, 1896, is a red-letter day, not only in the history of automobilism, but in that of England itself, for it marks the throwing open of the highways and byeways of our beautiful country to those who elect to travel thereupon in carriages propelled by motors, instead of in horse-drawn vehicles or upon bicycles. And how better can we celebrate the occasion than by making it a "red-letter day" in fact for *The Autocar*, seeing how great a share *The Autocar* has had in obtaining for autocarists this great concession, which, but for the curious and illogical reasonings of the legal mind, and benighted legislation of former years, would never have had to be obtained by Act of Parliament from a more enlightened Government, but would have fallen to us freely as a natural and inalienable right.

"THE MOTOR CAR SPECIAL."

In the meantime a special train had been chartered, consisting of some ten or fifteen saloon carriages, in which the invited guests of the club were taken to Reigate. Just by Coulsdon, where the rail for a short period runs within sight of the high road, a view was obtained of some of the foremost autocars, the first intimation of their presence being the sight of a Bollée car making rapid headway with a horseman in front, evidently endeavouring to get away from it. The horseman was soon done with, and the train party saw him draw his animal back in a considerably heated condition. Then the Duryea car was sighted and another Bollée, and by the time Reigate was reached, after several slows and stoppages, three of the speedy carriages had already passed through, having beaten the L.B. & S.C.R. special.

REIGATE.

As we turned out of the train at Reigate we began to realise how bad the rain had made the roads. Nobody ran down to the "White Hart," but everyone wanted to, as all were keen to get to the road to see the carriages, and so we padd'ed through the dirt as fast as dignity would allow. We found Reigate in a state of uproar, thousands of people, with just a narrow lane through the midst of them, down which a single line of traffic felt its way with difficulty. We had no sooner struggled into a front place than up came the Bollée with Duncan at the helm and Turrell, sen., at the prow. They went through without stopping, scorning food. Here we found that the other two Bollées were out for speed, and had gone straight on from Redhill. A few minutes later the Panhard and Levassor vehicle, the winner of the recent Paris-Marseilles contest, passed through, then came the Peugeot omnibus, followed by a couple of Duryeas. These two smart-looking American vehicles were without splash-guards, and the two occupants of each were carrying enough mud on their hats, faces, and clothes to start a small estate. Then Mr. Lawson in the pilot car came through with his banner flying, and the good people of Reigate cheering lustily. Mr. C. M. R. Turrell drove in soon after, and Mr. Crowden passed through at the helm of the Panhard waggonette, the second vehicle in the Paris-Marseilles contest. We had most of us forgotten to obtain food, so hastily securing some pocket sustenance, we tore back to the station and boarded the "special," quite envying the crowds we left behind us. We were struck with the intense interest taken in the autocars by the thousands of cyclists, both ladies and gentlemen, who braved the bad roads and congested traffic to follow and, if the truth must be told, to hamper the drivers of the carriages, as the pedal-pushers were so numerous that it was often a work of art to steer clear of them, and we think it little short of marvellous that no accident occurred. It certainly speaks volumes for the ease with which the horseless vehicles can be steered and stopped.

Excerpts from the motoring press on the day of the Run and a week later.

The car is a Victoria Combination made in 1900 in Paris. The little car had front wheel drive and centre-pivot steering, so the engine turned with the steering. The motor is a $3\frac{1}{2}$hp Aster. The couple pose outside 5 and 7 Thicket Crescent, Sutton.

A 1902 6½hp Locomobile outside Ewell Grove the home of Sir David Evans KCMG who was Lord Mayor of London in 1891-1892 and the first Welshman to hold that position. Lady Evans is being driven by her son, Ianto Evans. The car was described as 'of the improved pattern with 16 inch boiler'.

The Locomobile was a successful steam-powered runabout with twin-cylinder simple engine and boiler under the seat. It was tiller-steered and drive was by a central chain to the rear differential. It is said that the boiler had to be refilled every twenty miles, so perhaps the large water condenser added below the dashboard was a necessary addition and gave extra range between water stops. The side basket is for umbrellas.
(Extracted from *Car Illustated Magazine* 1904.)

'Blackstone' is on Redhill Common, off White Post Hill, and the copse of trees is still there. The cars from the left are: A-867 – Panhard et Levassor, A-5010 – Panhard et Levassor, P-1310 and P-119 – De Dion Boutons (P-119 still exists), P-9? – Dennis or Darracq, P-64 – unidentified forecar, P-114 De Dion Bouton motorcycle – perhaps an Alldays, P-3 unidentified motorcycle – probably a Rex, P-470 – Panhard et Levassor, P-147 – Wolseley, P-275 – The author's 1900 Benz, P-17? – Wolseley, ? – Panhard et Levassor. The 1900 Benz, then fours years old, is the oldest car in the picture. It was bought from the Sevenoaks Motor Agency and Stores on 15

September 1900 by Dr C.F. Wakefield of Lincoln Lodge, Horsehills, Horley. It cost £205 16s 0d complete with hood and apron. It has a single-cylinder horizontal engine driving the rear axle by belts and chains. The author bought it from Dr Wakefield's son in 1957 and collected it from Norwood Hill with a borrowed Ferguson tractor and trailer. His family has kept the car in use since, meaning that the car has lived for over one hundred years in the same borough and had only two owners.

June 15, 1904.

THE EAST SURREY A.C.

THE opening run of the season of the above club brought out a very good muster. The members were invited to lunch at "Blackstone," Redhill, the residence of Mr. J. B. Purchase, and about fifty members availed themselves of the invitation. After submitting to the ordeal of the camera, the members proceeded by various routes to "Timberham," Charlwood, the residence of Mr. F. E. Charles, who entertained the party to tea.

A very pleasant afternoon was spent here, and the run altogether proved a most enjoyable one. Among those who took part in the run were :—Major Kingsley O. Foster (president), Mr. and Mrs. J. B. Purchase and party, Mr. and Mrs. E. K. Purchase, Mr. and Mrs. F. E. Charles and party, Mr. C. H. Whittington, Mr. and Mrs. A. Gunning Keen, Mr. J. Underhill and party, Mr. and Mrs. G. H. Bowden, Mr. H. Hughes, Mr. and Mrs. C. F. Wakefield, Mr. F. W. Ellwood, Dr. J. Hewetson and Mr. Frank Watney, Mr. H. Rosling and party, Mr. A. W. Makovski and party, Mr. J. Humphrey and party, Mr. and Mrs. W. Cleaver and party, Mr. W. F. Garside, Mr. D. J. Barry (honorary secretary), and Mrs. Barry.

THE ADMINISTRATIVE COUNTY OF SURREY.

THE MOTOR CAR ACTS, 1896 & 1903.

COPY OF ENTRIES IN REGISTER OF MOTOR CARS.

Index Mark and Number on Identification Plates.	Full Name of Owner and Postal Address of his usual Residence.	Description or Type of Car.	Type and Colour of Body of Car.	Weight unladen.	Whether intended for—			Date of Registration.	If Cancelled, Date of Cancellation.
					(a) Private use.	(b) Use for Trade Purposes.	(c) Use for a Public Conveyance.		
1	2	3	4	5	6			7	8
P 275.	Wakefield Christopher Frank. Lincoln Lodge. Horley.	3. H.P. Benz Car.	Victoria 3 seated. Dark Green + Black Hood.	15 cwt.	Yes			21 ... 1903.	

Extracted from the Register

.... Clerk of the Council.

A fine French 16 hp De Dietrich of 1903. The engine had four cylinders, the gearbox had four speeds worked by a quadrant gear lever and final drive was by side chains. The owner, Mr Macaulay Mort of South Park, Haslemere recorded that 'the magneto ignition seems perfect and has given me no trouble. An incidental advantage is the absence of accumulators, which has allowed me to fit a large box on the step. In this I carry spare inner tubes, jack, pump and repair outfit.' Other tools were housed in the box below the tonneau at the back of the car.

The quadrant gearchange meant that the lever worked in one line selecting reverse – neutral –1 – 2 – 3 – 4. There was no synchro-mesh and when slowing down it was not possible to get from top gear to bottom without double-declutching through third and second.

Ignition initially was often by 'hot-tube' involving a petrol-flame below a platinum tube with its other end in the cylinder head but disadvantages included the flame blowing out and that no ignition timing was possible. Before 1900 ignition became electric either by battery and trembler coils or by magneto. The magneto generates electric current when it is rotated.

The De Dietrich shown has a rear-entrance tonneau body and detachable canopy top.

THE RENOWNED
DE DIETRICH
(French Made).

24-h.p. TOURING CAR.

NO TROUBLE WITH MACHINERY.　　**IGNITION PERFECT.**

Sir PHILIP F. ROSE, Bart., writes—

Rayners Penn,
Dear Mr. Jarrott,　　　　　　　　Bucks, July 14th, 1903.
　　In answer to your enquiries about my 16-h.p. De Dietrich, I can only speak in the highest terms of it. I have never had the least trouble with its machinery, and the ignition system seems to me perfect. It has been greatly admired wherever it has been, and I suppose I must by now have run a good deal over 1,000 miles in it.
　　I shall certainly recommend my friends to go in for De Dietrich Cars. One possessor of another 16-h.p. car, who saw my car at a garden party last week, said he should certainly sell his car and get one like mine.—Yours faithfully,
　　　　　　　　　　　　　　(Signed)　PHILIP F. ROSE.

THREE　PERFECT　MODELS.
12 H.P.　　　16 H.P.　　　24 H.P.
(Four Cylinders.)

MM. DE DIETRICH & Cᴵᴱ., PARIS.

Full particulars, specifications, and appointments for trial on application to our Sole English Concessionnaires—

CHARLES JARROTT & LETTS, Ltd., 45, GREAT MARLBOROUGH STREET, REGENT STREET, W.

Sutton Place, near Guildford, was built in the reign of Henry VIII. We might remember it as the home of oil billionaire Jean Paul Getty, but in 1903 it was the home of Alfred Harmsworth (later Lord Northcliffe, d.1922) the newspaper magnate. In *The Car Illustrated* magazine of 29 April 1903, the Hon. J.S. Montagu wrote 'Except for the proximity to the neighbourhood in which Sergeant Jarrott and the Surrey magistrates reign supreme, Sutton Place is an ideal home for a motorist.' This is a reference to the police trapping of motorists at the time being particularly antagonistic in west Surrey.

Alfred Harmsworth had owned many cars prior to April 1903 when these pictures were taken. It was a time when no-one was certain that the petrol engine would prove better than electricity or steam. Here we have all three!

Opposite page, top right: The upper car is a Mercedes petrol-engined car of 28hp but using electric front-wheel-drive units designed by Lohner Porsche. The use of two electric motors obviated the need for a differential. Jacob Lohner and Ferdinand Porsche were both Austrians. One contemporary report suggested that pulling by the front wheels must be right as it was similar to horse-drawn vehicles!

Ferdinand Porsche was later to be known as the 'father of Volkswagen' a car he designed for Hitler in the thirties. Born in Bohemia in 1875 he worked for Jacob Lohner from 1896 to 1906 as a battery-electric and then petrol-electric vehicle designer.

Bottom right:
The lower car is a French Serpollet steam car of 40hp. At the front is the steam condenser, and the bonnet covers only the water reservoir. The fuel tank is below the driver's seat and the engine is placed horizontally below the rear floor driving the rear axle by a single chain. The boiler is outside the rear of the car with the curved cowl above it serving to deflect flames away from the folded hood!

The chassis and engine of the Gardner-Serpollet in the lower picture opposite.

A Panhard et Levassor of c.1904, perhaps the three-cylinder model and fitted with a limousine body awaits its owner. On the roof is an extending ladder used to gain access to luggage carried on the roof. It was more usual to have a folding ladder that could be stowed beneath the back seat. Charles Rolls first met Henry Royce in May 1904 and Rolls-Royce was born. Here is Rolls' advert for new Panhards and other cars secondhand only a few months earlier.

On the next three pages are some of Surrey's Panhards of the period.

Mr J.F. Wright outside his home Frimley Hall. The ladies in the tonneau are veiled ready for an outing. The car is another 10hp four-cylinder Panhard et Levassor but this time with varnished wood body with turned spindle decoration. The car was registered P-53 and was Mr Wright's second Panhard, the first being a 7hp two-cylinder model. Frimley Hall, north of Aldershot Common, stood in seventy acres of grounds which included a nine-hole golf course.

The French Panhard et Levassor was a popular choice in 1903 and the British agent was the Hon. Charles Rolls. This one is of 10hp with a four cylinder engine. There are brackets for a hood above the rear seats, but when they are fitted and lowered access to the back through the central rear door was not easy. Folded up against the rear door is a central seat. When this is lowered between the corner seats it completes the row and the door cannot open.

The car belonged to the Earl of Onslow, then the Minister of Agriculture, and is seen at his country house Clandon Park in west Surrey. The house now belongs to the National Trust.

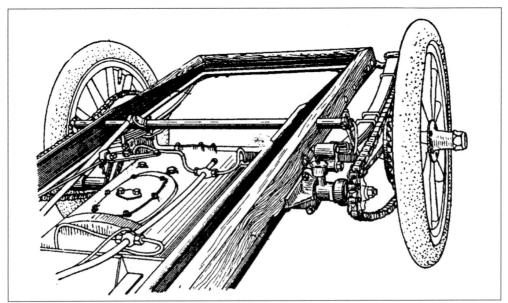

The gearbox and final chain-drive of an early Panhard et Levassor. The chassis is steel with strengthening wooden flitch-plates.

Another Panhard et Levassor, but a 15hp, four cylinder car. It still has rear seat entrance at the back. The superb oval headlamps are brass and used acetylene crystals to generate light. The side-lamps are oil. BY-1 was the first number issued by the County Borough of Croydon in December 1903, prior to registrations coming into law on 1 January 1904. This does not mean it was the earliest car in Croydon – it wasn't – but that Mr Preston of Shirley Hurst, Shirley was the first to apply to the Borough Council for a number.

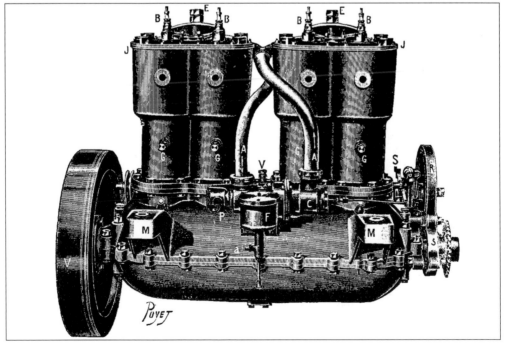

A drawing of the Panhard et Levassor engine.

The Rochet-Schneider was made at Lyons, France, from 1894 to 1932 and this one is of 20/22hp and 1903. It really looks quite conventional with all wheels the same size, a normal looking radiator and a side entrance to the generous rear seats. The car also has a hood covering all the occupants. The car belonged to Mr W. Marden of Ockenshaw, Surbiton.

The Chenard et Walcker was made in the Hauts de Seine area, west of Paris, from 1901 to 1939. This car is of 1904; the 10hp car used a separate cardan shaft for each rear wheel. The driver is Mr Berna Frith of Croydon and the picture is dated 1 December 1904.

An uncommon make was the Brooke, made at Lowestoft pre-First World War. The 14hp engine had three cylinders. Brookes usually had a bowl in the middle of the steering wheel to hold gloves, goggles or other items. This one dates from 1903.

Russ Hill, Charlwood, just above Gatwick was the home of Mr H.N. Corsellis who had a stable of four Germains in 1904. This one had a 15hp engine and a removable brougham top in addition to the hood shown here. Earlier in 1904 Mr Corsellis took this car and his 1904 16hp Germain (P-474) to Biarritz and then San Sebastian and back.

The Actresses' Motor Meet on 22nd June 1903 at the Oatlands Park Hotel, Weybridge. The two cars in the centre are Daimlers. The white car was entered by E.M.C. Instone, the manager of the Daimler company in Coventry so he is probably busy demonstrating it to a customer.

The Milnes-Daimler was a German Daimler with body by Milnes of Wellington, Shropshire, who were normally tram constructors. Milnes-Daimler made many buses and lorries in the first seven years of the last century, but cars only at the beginning.

This is Mr H.G. Burford's 1903 car at Hindhead for the timing of a hill-climb of the ACGBI 1,000 Mile Trial in September 1903. The standing timekeepers are Mr J. Lyons Sampson and Mr J.F. Ochs, and sitting beside Mr Burford is Col. R.B. Crompton.

The day's run was $144\frac{1}{2}$ miles from London to Southsea and back on Wednesday 23 September 1903. It was part of the One Thousand Mile Trial of that year organised by the ACGBI, later to become the RAC.

Shelvey & Co. soft drinks of Guildford put this Brighton-registered Milnes-Daimler lorry in its fleet in 1903/4. The lorry had started life as a Southdown bus!

"A USEFUL LITTLE CAR."

This Car is manufactured by the

GENERAL MOTOR CAR Co., Ltd.,

OF

LONDON ROAD, NORBURY, S.W.,

AND

MITCHAM COMMON, SURREY.

It was designed especially to suit the requirements of Doctors and other Professional Gentlemen, and although only recently introduced has gained considerable popularity.

The Price is 165 Guineas.

The General Motors Corporation was formed in America in 1908.

This company tried various manufactures between 1902 and 1905 varying from a 40hp General racing car, with a pointed front several feet ahead of the front axle, to vans supplied to the Post Office.

Horley survived from 1904 until 1909 starting with an 8 hp MMC (Motor Manufacturing Co. of Coventry) single-cylinder engine and priced at one hundred guineas, though the ones shown above at the February 1904 Crystal Palace Show are both four seaters with rear entrance. A month later, at London's Agricultural Hall, two vans are offered for an extra £30. The van on the left can have its rear body removed and replaced with the rear seats and centre door unit shown to the left. Horley were agents for a French company, Lacoste et Battman, who supplied all sorts of car components and even complete cars, so it is likely that the Horley used many such parts. For part of its short life Horley cars were also sold as No Names.

THE SORT OF QUESTION WE ENJOY!

Curious Onlooker : Now, mister, how far do yer reckon your car'll go wi' just that one turn o' that there 'andle ?

W. Leeding & Sons Ltd traded from 109 High Street, Sutton, having previously been Sutton Carriage Works. The earliest car shown is an American White steam car of 1903 or 1904, the steam controls on the floor and the enormous condenser radiator are features. The solid rubber rear tyres are unusual. The rear body is made to fold away under two covers to create a two seater car with a luggage platform.

The French Renault below is 1904 model UB or UC of four cylinders and 3,050cc, giving 14hp. It marked an important modernisation for Renault, being the first car to have its radiator across behind the bonnet instead of at the sides (this radiator has a flat top). This bonnet and radiator styling would remain a feature of Renaults for twenty-five years. The car has a tubular chassis and a rear-entrance tonneau body with 'tulip-styling'. It was registered 'A' in London in 1904.

A proud Reigate man, Bertram Finch, who created the family bicycle shop that still flourishes in Bell Street, Reigate, in the hands of his great-grandson. He rides a c.1903 Brown, with basket forecar with a single-cylinder 498cc engine. Why the vehicle carries a 1905 rather than 1904 registration is a mystery. Brown Bros also still trade as motor parts factors. They made (or sold as their own) motor cycles, tricycles and cars from 1901 until the First World War.

Later to make cars under his own name, Herbert Austin was general manager at Wolseley from 1896 to 1905, during which time nearly all Wolseley engines were horizontal transverse to the chassis and with only the cylinder heads, valve gear and carburettor visible on opening the bonnet lid. It was also usual for them to have an inverted tooth chain driving the gearbox and chain drive to the two back wheels. This is a 6hp single-cylinder Wolseley of 1905 and it has a single chain drive to the differential of the back axle. The engine has a $4\frac{1}{2}$in by 5in bore and stroke and runs up to 1,000rpm. At 800rpm it developed 6bhp. The car was owned by Mr and Mrs Riff Willis who lived in Merton.

An advertisement at the end of 1904 shows a trade-plate registration 'O' being for Birmingham and 'WY' for the Wolseley Co.

Weighty Gentleman (who owns the tandem): What's the matter? How is it you don't start? Can't you set it going? You're making plenty of noise !!!

His Invited Friend: I don't know. . . . I think the beastly thing 'mistakes me for an aeronaut!

Mr H.H. Longman, the publisher, lived at Lavershot Hall, Windlesham, near Sunningdale, and kept this 16hp Dennis as well as a small Panhard.

Dennis Bros of Guildford made many cars in the early 1900s and this one dates from 1905. All Dennises from this date featured overhead worm-drive rear axles. This car probably has an Aster engine, but from 1906 White and Poppe engines were used. The rear entrance body, even though with four comfortable corner seats, was a bit dated by 1905 and this chassis is long enough to have allowed a side-entrance body.

At the time of this picture, the Reigate Garage, later well-known in Bell Street, had its premises just north of the level-crossing on the corner of Somers Road.

The top-hatted customer on the left holds a side-entrance 1905 Darracq and on the right is a De Dion Bouton of the same date.

Above and Opposite:
The American 20hp Winton had a two-cylinder engine and two-speed planetary transmission.
The car was known in America as a roadster. The rear tonneau seats were detachable (along
the diagonal line on the lower body side).

The car belonged to Maj. Gen. Sir Henry and Lady Colville of Lightwater, Bagshot, and the
Winton was bought by them at the February 1905 Olympia Motor Show.

Exactly a year later, Sir Henry Colville exchanged his 20/24 Winton for the new 'K' model
Winton with four cylinders and 5.8 litres but only two forward speeds. The spring shapes are
perhaps unique to Wintons of this period. This car also has support brackets for a Surrey roof.

The Sage was made in Paris from 1900 to 1906 only. This one is campaigning for 'Chaplin for Wimbledon' inside the spare cover which is a metal-studded non-skid tyre. Although the Stepney wheel rim was available from 1904, one is not fitted. The car is from 1906 and is still chain driven. Note that the chain is exposed, with merely a step-plate above it, meaning ladies in the long dresses of the period would have taken care getting in.

The first Rover four-wheeler was an 8hp single-cylinder car introduced in 1904. It had a backbone chassis with the unusual feature for the time of the gearbox being in unit with the engine. The steering column gear-change can be seen. For this four-seater the access to the back was through the front as the front passenger's seat tipped over to the side.

One wonders what the bell hanging from the wing bracket did! Perhaps it gave warning if a large flint or broken horse-shoe was picked up but one would have to stop very quickly to prevent damaging tyre and tube.

Number plates are misleading. P-2037 was subsequently re-registered P-5247 although only its first owner lived in Surrey. The very first Rolls-Royce 10hp car which left the then Manchester works in September 1904 was registered P-200 and may have been used by Mr Percy Northey of The Cottage, Ashtead Park, who joined Rolls-Royce in 1905 and in the same year came second in the Tourist Trophy Race on the Isle of Man in a 20hp Rolls-Royce.

The smaller Rolls-Royce P-2037 with park phaeton body by Barker & Co. (London) was sold to Mr Julian Whittington of Holmwood in the summer of 1905. In 1906 he lived at Sandhills, Betchworth. It was a 10hp two-cylinder car. Alongside is Julian Whittington's second Rolls-Royce P-2813. This is a 30hp six-cylinder car with body, again, by Barker, but this time a tourer with a detachable brougham top bought in the summer of 1906. Mr Whittington bought yet another Rolls Royce, a Silver Ghost, in 1913.

WEST SURREY AUTOMOBILE CLUB.

**A well-known member of the Club.
Mr. James F. Ochs.**

This club was formed in April, 1903, at a meeting called by the Rev. A. Armitage (now hon. secretary of the Somerset Automobile Club) and Mr. R. W. Buttemer, the present hon. secretary. The club has had a successful career. Club repairers have been appointed at Guildford, Farnham, Godalming, and Elstead.

OFFICE BEARERS.

President :
(Vacant).

Vice-President :
SIR A. CONAN DOYLE, Undershaw, Hindhead, Haslemere.

COMMITTEE:

Chairman :
COL. F. HOWARD FAIRTLOUGH, Hurtmore Holt, Godalming.

Treasurer :
MR. W. G. CROTHERS, Edgcumbe, Guildford.

MR. WILSON NOBLE, Tangley Park, Guildford
MR. J. F. W. PONSFORD, The Gate House, Shackleford, Godalming

MR. E. E. PULLMAN, Alverstoke, Clandon Road, Guildford
MR. A. C. Tessier, Edgehill, Guildford

Hon. Secretary :
MR. R. W. BUTTEMER, St. Mary's, Godalming (Telegrams : "Buttemer, Eashing.")

Head-quarters : The ANGEL HOTEL, Guildford (Telephone : 0187, Guildford).

Representatives on the Committee of the Motor Union :
COL. HOWARD FAIRTLOUGH and MR. R. W. BUTTEMER.

Affiliated : A.C.G.B.I. 1903.   Established : April 28th, 1903.   Subscription : £1 10s.
No entrance fee.

MEMBERS (in addition to those above).

Armitage, E., Tilford, Farnham.

Baring-Gould, E., Box Grove House, Guildford.
Baring-Gould, F., Merrow Grange, Guildford.
Barker, S., Grayswood Tower, Haslemere.
Bashall, H. St. J., Elm Grove, Ockham.
Broderick, Rt. Hon. W. St. J., Peper Harow, Godalming.
Bryden, Dr. F. W., The Priory, Godalming.
Bullerd, Mrs., Frolbury Manor, Dorking.

Chance, Sir W., Orchards, Godalming.
Cowan, W. H., Tangley Hill, Chilworth.
Cox, G. P., Stone House, Godalming.

Fennings, Dr. A., The Vines, Farncombe, Godalming.
Fletcher, J. S., Heathfield, East Molesey.

Gouldsbury, Col. D., The Beeches, Woking.

Halahan, G. C., Old Pickhurst, Chiddingford, Godalming.
Hall, Dr. G., Windham Lodge, Milford, Godalming.
Hambro, H. C., Hampton Lodge, Seale, Farnham.
Henderson, Dr., Kinnoull, Warwick's Bench, Guildford.
Hook, B., Beefolds, Churt, Farnham.
Horniman, E. J., Lowicks, Farnham.
Houghton, F., Cranley Lodge, Guildford.
Houghton, W. C., Ridge End, Woking.

Ingram, C., Elstead House, Godalming.

Jenkinson, Miss M., Thurlow, Godalming.

King, A., Rexholme, Edgeboro' Rd., Guildford.
King, J., Sandhouse, Witley.
Knight, J. H., Barfield, Farnham.

Leon, A., Stoatley Rough, Haslemere.

McCaskill, R., The Beeches, Addlestone.
Matson, Major C. J., Watford, Guildford.
Mitchell, Dr., St. Vincent's, Epsom Rd., Guildford.

Montagu, Major A. W., Denham House, Guildford.

O'Callaghan, Sir F., Crichmere, Edgeborough Rd., Guildford.
Ochs, J. F., St. Ann's Hill, Chertsey.

Praschkauer, M., Theobalds, Chilworth.
Price, A. R., 2, White Lion Court, Cornhill, E.C.
Price, H. S., Broadwater, Godalming.

Rawstorne, Col., Old Croft, Shalford, Guildford.
Raxworthy, H., Tuesley, Godalming.
Rideal, Dr. S., The Chalet, Elstead.
Robertson, R. S., Meadrow House, Farncombe, Godalming.
Roumieu, G. F., Bathune House, Farnham.

Sartorius, Col. G. C., Thorwald, Godalming.
Sichel, G., Eastfield Lodge, Epsom Rd., Guildford.
Simmonds, R., The Elms, Aldershot.
Simmons, G. A., Woburn Hill, Addlestone.
Smith, Dr. G., High Down, Hindhead.
Swinscow, F. W., Faringcote, Pewley Hill, Guildford.

Thorne-Thorne, Dr. B., Grasmere, Woking.
Thorne-Thorne, Dr. R., Essendene, Chobham Rd., Woking.
Treatt, R. C., Mill House, Elstead, Godalming.
Tringham, Capt. A., Stoughton Barracks, Guildford.
Turnor, C., Berthorpe, Compton, Guildford.

Vogan, R., The Beeches, Guildown, Guildford.

Warne, S., Frolbury Manor, Dorking.
Williams, E., Rydeshill House, Guildford.
Wrigley, O. O., Shackleford, Godalming.
Wyatt-Smith, Dr. F., Briarwood, Woking.

Club
membership
in 1905

EAST SURREY AUTOMOBILE CLUB.

This Club was formed on May 30th, 1903, for the encouragement and development of mechanically-propelled vehicles in the district of East Surrey, and takes in the whole of that district, but motorists who do not reside in the county are not debarred from becoming honorary members. Several very successful meets and runs were held in 1905, and the membership showed very satisfactory increase. The club has excellently-situated head-quarters at the White Hart Hotel, where an inspection pit and petrol-store have been constructed; while there is also ample accommodation under cover for cars, and a separate room can be had for chauffeurs at a fixed, inclusive charge, if necessary.

The President, Major Kingsley O. Foster, J.P., C.C.,

OFFICE BEARERS.

President:
*MAJOR KINGSLEY O. FOSTER, J.P., C.C., Shenley, Redhill.

Vice-Presidents:
SIR A. RENDEL, 8, Great George Street, Westminster, London, S.W.
SIR G. LIVESEY, C.E., Shagbrook, Reigate Heath
*CAPT. R. H. RAWSON, D.L., J.P. SUSSEX, Woodhurst, Crawley, Sussex.

*MR. H. N. CORSELLIS, Russ Hill, Charlwood
MR. H. BELL, Mynthurst, Leigh

COMMITTEE.

MR. G. H. BOWDEN, F.P.S., Roseneath, Reigate
MR. N. COLMAN, Nork Park, Epsom Downs
MR. A. GUNNING KEEN, 8, Yorke Road, Reigate
MR. H. HUGHES, Fairleigh, Reigate
MR. A. MACAIRE, West Street, Reigate
*MR. J. B. PURCHASE, Blackstone, Redhill
DR. W. F. GARSIDE, Oakley, Reigate

*MR. J. UNDERHILL, Clovelly, Upper Warlingham
DR. C. F. WAKEFIELD, M.R.C.S., Lincoln Lodge, Horley
*MR. C. H. WHITTINGTON, Sandhills, Betchworth
MR. H. ROSLING, Jun., Redleafe, Pilgrim's Way, Reigate

Honorary Auditor:
*MR. E. A. MERCER, Evesham Road, Reigate.

Honorary Secretary and Treasurer:
MR. DAVID J. BARRY, C.E., 50, High Street, Reigate.

Head-quarters:
WHITE HART HOTEL, Reigate.

Representatives on the General Committee of the Motor Union:
MR. DAVID J. BARRY, C.E.   MR. G. H. BOWDEN.

Representatives on the General Council of the A.C.G.B.I.
MAJOR KINGSLEY O. FOSTER, J.P.   MR. J. B. PURCHASE.

The Club Badge.

Established: May 30th, 1903. Subscription, for original members, £1 11s. 6d.; for ordinary members, £1 11s. 6d., entrance fee, £1 1s. od. Lady members. Subscription, £1 1s. od., no entrance fee. Affiliated: A.C.G.B.I., September, 1903, and Motor Union.

MEMBERS. (In addition to above.)

Amsden, E., Shirley, nr. Croydon.
Amsden, Mrs. B., Shirley, nr. Croydon.
Barry, D. J., C.E., Ledbury, Reigate.
Benson, A., Upper Gatton Park, Merstham.
*Boulter, R. S. L., Garston Park, Godstone.
*Campbell, R. E., Charlwood, Park, Charlwood.
Charles, F., Timberham, Charlwood.
Cleaver, W., The Rock, Reigate.
Ellwood, F. H., Granville House, Redhill.
Few, H. G., Haversham House, Putney, S.W.

Low, T. V., Holt House, Redhill.

Makovski, A. W., A.M.I.E.E., Rosery Cottage, Redhill.
Marcus, M., High Trees, Redhill.
Mercer, E. A., Evesham Rd., Reigate.
Messenger, S. J., Heathfield, Reigate.
Mott, P. L., Morden Grange, Betchworth.

Prince, P., B.A., M.R.C.S., Egremont, Somers Rd., Reigate.

Fisher, J. A., Steinholme, Warlingham.
George, Major F. N., Lovell House, Crawley.
Goad, E. H., Castle Keep, Reigate.
Hart, F., Owden, Mulgrave House, Sutton.
Hewetson, Dr. J., Holmfield, Reigate.
Horne, F. N., Colley Manor, Reigate.
Hull, L. S. B., Earlswood Mount, Redhill.
Humphery, J. H., Reigate.
Kempe, H. R., North Lodge, Brockham Green, Reigate.
*Lewis, H., Vron Dirion, Harewood Rd., South Croydon.

Rawson, Lady B., Woodhurst, Crawley. Sussex.
Scrutton, J. H., White House, Buckland.
Stone, H. S., B.A., M.B., Beechwood, Reigate.
Whittington, A. R., Sandhills, Betchworth.
Whittington, R., Sandhills, Betchworth.
Whittington, J., Sandhills, Betchworth.
Whittington, Miss W., Sandhills, Betchworth.

* Members of A.C.G.B.I.

Club membership in 1905

An American Cadillac of *c.* 1907, but the Surrey registration is nearly ten years later so the picture is post-First World War. This model has a single-cylinder horizontal engine under the floor in the centre of the vehicle, two-speed planetary gears and rear drive by a central chain to the differential. The bonnet is false but fitted to keep the model looking up-to-date.

Stepney spare wheel.

Pre-1914 roads were mostly just rolled stones covered by pulverised horse-droppings which made for ammonia-laden dust in summer and a white covering of slime on the verges in wet weather. Veteran cars had many punctures from sharp stones, broken horse-shoes and bent horse-shoe nails. Early wheels were non-detachable so the mending of punctures at the side of the road was an integral part of car travel.

The introduction of the Stepney wheel (not made in London but from Llanelli, in south Wales) permitted a ready-inflated tyre to be carried on a rim attachable to any of the cars wheels.

The sound of the Pick is heard no more,
and the Roller is at rest.

There is no detail of date or location to this postcard but it was sent with best wishes from Aunt Amy. The roads before Tarmacadam was generally used were often in this state.

THE PILGRIMS WAY MOTOR CO., LTD., FARNHAM, SURREY.

SILVER MEDAL IN TOWN MOTOR CARRIAGE COMPETITION. 1906 1906

GOLD MEDAL IN VAPOUR EMISSION COMPETITION. 1907 1907

32-H.P. " PILGRIM " (R.A.C. RATING).

From 1906 to 1908 the Pilgrim's Way Motor Co. Ltd. of Farnham made the Pilgrim car. This one, registered P-332?, is of 1907 and has a 5 1/2 litre four-cylinder engine located horizontally across the middle of the chassis. The two-speed epicyclic gearbox connects to the rear axle by one central chain. The layout allowed a large body on a short chassis. After a receivership in 1908 there were more Pilgrims made from 1911 to 1914.

The Lagonda Co.'s address was Staines but the factory was on the Surrey side of the bridge, so they were Surrey-made cars until both Lagonda and Aston-Martin were taken over by the David Brown organisation in 1947. Lagondas were created by Wilbur Gunn who came to England from Ohio and the name originates from the American-Indian name of Lagonda Creek where he had been brought up. V-twin engined forecars were made from 1900 and four-wheel cars added from 1906.

This picture was taken during the Sunbeam Motor Cycle Club's Third Pioneer Run in 1932. The Run started from the goods yard of Tattenham Station and finished at the Aquarium Garage on Brighton front. George Burtenshaw's car is being attended by an AA man while his daughter looks on. (She is also shown with the Chrysler Croydon on page 118 and her looks were said to be an asset to the business).

Mr Burtenshaw had won a Gold Cup at the Lagonda Rally in 1930 and driven in the Lord Mayor of London's Show in 1931. The car was thought to date from 1904 but, as this forecar with 9hp, wheel-steering and water-cooling (the header tank is below the passenger's elbow) were not introduced until 1906, the date must accord with the registration, LN-3252 which puts it at early 1907.

Also said to date from 1907 is the 10hp Croydon-registered Lagonda forecar BY-1124 of Miss Ivy Mitchell, driving in the Auto-Cycle Union's Quarterly Trial in April 1909 based at Uxbridge. It was reported that 'her engine was running rather fitfully and she retired after Dashwood Hill'. Below it is a similar Lagonda owned by William Toms, a nurseryman, and here seen in his garden at Heathview, Banstead Road, Caterham.

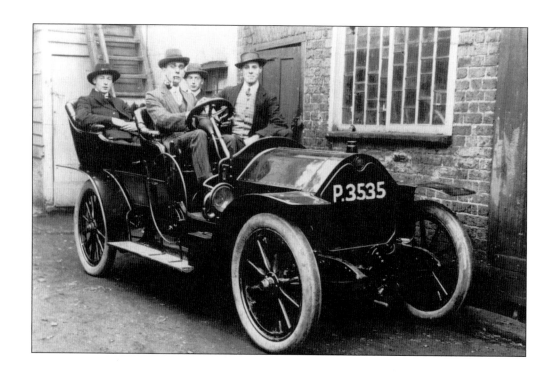

This Darracq four-cylinder side-entrance tourer of *c.*1908 is driven by George Burtenshaw, coachbuilder of West Street, Reigate. Early Darracqs had steering-column gear-change levers. It was a Darracq of 1904/5 that Kenneth More drove as *Genevieve* in the 1955 film.

S.F. Edge was born in Sydney, Australia but was at school in Upper Norwood. He then worked in the budding tyre trade but in 1900 persuaded Montague Napier to enter the car business. Edge won the 1902 Gordon Bennett Race in a Napier, and in 1907 he drove single-handed for twenty-four hours round the newly-built Brooklands Track. He covered over 1,581 miles at an average speed of 65.9mph.

Edge is seen here with an L48 Napier which he used for practising night-driving in June 1907 prior to the Twenty-Four Hour Run. The newly built track and the slope soon to be the Test Hill can be seen behind the car.

At the first meeting to discuss the size, shape, etc. of the proposed Brooklands track, Edge caused astonishment by asking to order it so soon as it was completed for his twenty-four hour drive. Below, the three 60hp Napiers await the start. Edge is on the left, Henry C. Tryon in the centre car, and Frank Newton on the right. The cars were coloured green, red and white and all three cars completed the twenty-four hours without any mechanical troubles at all.

The Hut Hotel used to be on the A3 at Wisley Common just on the London side of the Royal Horticultural Society's gardens. The Hut faced the lake called Bolder Mere and its foundations must now be under the dual carriageway.

From the left are a two-cylinder Darracq (P-4050), a two-cylinder Riley 12/18 with oval radiator (DU-1885), a Stanley steamer (on trade plates CN-G-6) a four-cylinder Talbot (LN-7790) belonging to Mr Toler, who stands behind his chauffeur. Next is a three-wheeler and then a single-cylinder Rover behind a scooter and another Surrey-registered three-wheeler (P-962). Two motorcycles then precede a Humber (LB-5885) and an unidentified little car with high-mounted acetylene headlight.

To the right is the Darracq seen on the left of the line-up above.

49

Back to Leedings coachbuilders of Sutton High Street, though the house is probably Mogeela in Worcester Road, Cheam, where the chauffeur poses beside Mr H.E. Renton's 1908 Vauxhall tourer. The 12/16hp four-cylinder engine had separately cast cylinders with T-heads. This was the first Vauxhall to have the bonnet flutes that would identify the make for the next fifty years.

Vauxhall had made boat steam engines in Vauxhall, London before making cars from 1903. In 1905 the company moved to Luton, and it was a Bedfordshire registration (BM) that was issued to this car before delivery.

Wm Leeding may only have been engineers to Mr Renton as the body appears to be a standard Vauxhall-bodied tourer.

In front of the Leedings works in Sutton. The front doors put this Wolseley a little later than the Vauxhall at about 1910. The body is a landaulette with a luggage gallery on the fixed part of the roof. There is a speaking tube beside the driver's ear so instructions can be given from the back. Below the doors is a Gabriel exhaust-driven multi-tone horn and the wheel rims on this car are detachable. The spare tyre (carried outside the chauffeur's non-opening door) was kept inflated on a rim. The punctured tyre and rim could thus be changed complete to obviate mending the tube and re-inflating the tyre at the side of the road. The notice above the door 'Pratts Motor Spirit' advertised the availability of two-gallon cans of petrol in the days before pump fuel – and all stored in a wooden building!

50

FOR HIRE

With Mark. J. Gentry's Compliments.

Outside substantial gates a Talbot taxi is shown. Passenger access is through the door alongside the single front seat and the rear roof folds too. A very smart vehicle.

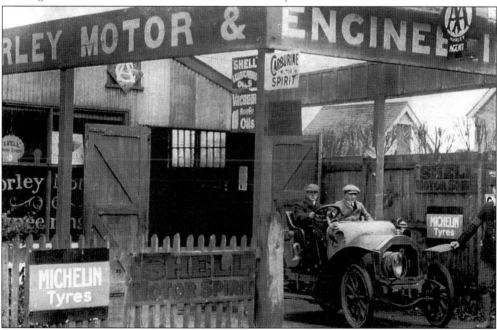

The Horley Motor & Engineering Co. building still stands facing the big roundabout with the Shell garage inside it on the A23 junction with Balcombe Road. The Horley company were also agents for Lacoste & Battmann, who were Parisian suppliers of major components for motor cars and many British makes were little more than badge-engineered Lacoste & Battmans. The car shown is a Mass, made in France but largely for the British market and largely comprising Lacoste & Battman components.

The Wolseley-Siddeley, above left is Middlesex registered in about 1909. Herbert Austin was general manager at Wolseley from its start in 1896 until 1905 when the company decided to depart from Austin's horizontal engines and adopt the vertical engines designed by J.D. Siddeley.

The Croydon-registered De Dion-Bouton on the right is a few years older and has the steering-column gear-change, alligator bonnet and low front radiator.

Below is another De Dion-Bouton of 1909, a four-cylinder 12hp two-seater with the new radiator style introduced in 1907.

Motor Engineers Chalmers and Co offered readers of this advertisement the latest in horseless carriages.

In horse-carriage days nearly every town had a coach builder and when cars came along the rich continued to order their own choice of bodies. Chalmers' advert shows their work on a French Delaunay Belleville chassis in 1909.

This 1909 Renault still survives! It is an example of the popular model AX. The bonnet opened alligator fashion which may be why the headlamps are not mounted. Behind the two-cylinder engine is the radiator whose filler cap can be seen at the top of it. The side-lamps are oil and these cars sometimes had a dickey seat where the chauffeur could travel if the owner wished to drive his wife.

In 1910, when these pictures were taken, Dennis Bros of Guildford reckoned they were Britain's oldest motor manufacturers, their first tricycles dating from 1895. From 1903 Dennis also made commercial vehicles and from 1904 all their products had Dennis worm-drive rear axles. Above is shown the Woodbridge factory at Guildford c.1909 with a Dennis turbine pump fire engine in the foreground and below is a 18hp tourer with electric side-lights. The awkward body waistline across the driver's side would be less obvious once a spare tyre or Stepney wheel was fitted. As is normal with all cars of this date, the gear-lever and hand-brake made an opening driver's door unnecessary.

The family chauffeur poses at the wheel of a Thornycroft landaulette of Basingstoke manufacture. The wire wheels are detachable and the spare wheel has a fitted cover. The acetylene headlights are oddly mounted on the wings but many Thornycroft cars display this feature. A mirror was rarely fitted pre-1914 even though the chauffeur's rearward visibility was almost nil.

The above car carries the wingless AA badge used up to 1911, whereas the cars below wear RAC badges from the club that received Royal patronage in 1907. The cars below are Léon Bollées from Le Mans in France. The high-mounted side-lights add to the impression that the cars may have been under the same ownership. It was 1907 before Leon Bollée introduced his first shaft-drive car, but some, such as the one on the left which is chain driven, were still made until 1910. This left-hand car also has a double-limousine body, double because not only the rear seats, but the front seats also, are completely enclosed.

The scuttle shape is typical of the 1910 date of this French 18/22hp Berliet, which was originally a tourer registered P-5407. It was converted to an ambulance in 1914 and went to France. In the early 1920s it was bought by Crow Bros of Guildford, the back converted to a breakdown truck and used as a works hack. For Crow family holidays the Berliet was loaded with bicycles, tents and luggage up until 1939 when the car was sent for scrap for £2 10s 0d. (The picture comes from A.D. Rubie, grandson of Charles Crow.)

From Croydon comes this Humber car. Humber cars up to the end of 1909 had single-spoke steering wheels, an invention that was to be announced by Citroen for the DS19 almost fifty years later! Humbers were made at Beeston (more expensively) and Coventry where this 15hp was built. The upper part of the body is detachable to leave the car as an open tourer.

What links the centre of Guildford with the centre of Cranleigh? In both cases the only car on the road is a Sunbeam. The Guildford car (P-3071) is a tourer of about 1910 and the Sunbeam in Cranleigh is an enclosed drive landaulette of perhaps one year later (P-4985).

Sunbeams were made at Wolverhampton until 1935 when the Sunbeam-Talbot-Darracq combine failed and was bought by the Rootes Group. Subsequent cars were Sunbeam-Talbots.

Outside Redhill Station is this landaulette. It is a Unic and likely to be a taxi. A Frenchman, Georges Richard, quit his partnership with Richard Brasier in 1905 to make what he intended to be a single model – hence Unic (unique). The Unic taxi was made for twenty years from 1908 and had a monobloc 12/14hp four-cylinder engine. Unics were a very common sight as taxis on London's streets.

In October 1910 the Austin and the Swift factories got together to make and market a single-cylinder 7hp two-seater car. This was the Swift and of the 1,030 vehicles they built over 900 were Swifts.

THE AUXILIARY SINGLE CABRIOLET.

Two cars from 1911, when Wolseley-Siddeleys reverted to being Wolseleys, and one from 1913. The one above was built as a single cabriolet for Mr Chas. Byworth of Lymescot, Benhilton Sutton, by Harris & Others of 65 Old Town, Clapham.

The upper car opposite is a similar 16/20hp Wolseley tourer with canvas bags over the lamps to keep the brass clean and an electric horn on the wing.

Below it is another tourer of a couple of years later. The marrying of the body line to the bonnet line has greatly improved. This is a car sold through Oaklands Park Motor Co. of Weybridge.

From 1911 Wolseleys were all equipped with wire-spoked wheels.

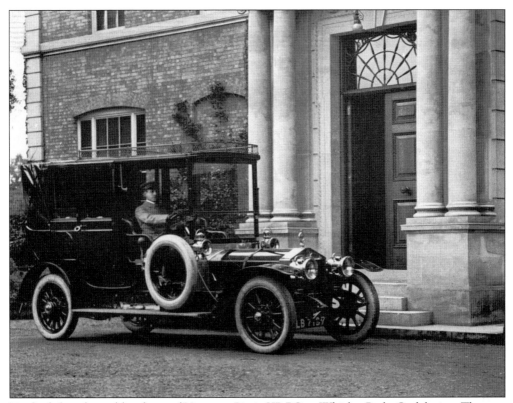

To the left is the stable of cars of Viscount Pirrie KP PC at Whitley Park, Godalming, The cars have London rather than Surrey registrations but there is no doubt that this is a Surrey-based garage-full.

The three Rolls-Royce Silver Ghosts on the left all have bodies by Morgan & Co. of Long Acre, London. The extraordinary – for the time – overhanging front wings of all the cars suggests that the Renault limousine, Renault landaulette and the Austin on the right were also bodied by Morgan.

Below left, the tourer is seen again. Not only the wings, but the double latching of the doors is better seen. Two Rolls-Royces date from 1910 and one (limousine) from 1911.

Above, on this page, is an earlier 1908 landaulette by Hooper on a Rolls-Royce Silver Ghost chassis. The chauffeur R.R. Thurlow is seen in front of Silverlands, Chertsey, the home of Sir John Brunner, M.P. for Northwich. The Silver Ghost was made as the company's only model from 1906 to 1925. It had a six-cylinder side-valve engine of 7,450cc. The leather bonnet strap was most unusual.

This Croydon-registered landaulette is a Fiat Type 1 of 1910-1912 and 12/15hp. The wheels are fitted with Warland detachable rims so that an inflated spare tyre could be carried making replacement after a puncture a cleaner and quicker job. (Note that the Rolls-Royce to the right also has Warland detachable wheel rims.) This Fiat is the smallest of the range having a four-cylinder engine of 1,846cc.

Mr Gordon Watney lived at South Lodge, Weybridge, where he specialised in the tuning and modifying of Mercedes cars to race at nearby Brooklands. Here he is seen, in cap, outside his house with seven such Mercedes cars, their drivers, and the 1911 haul of trophies. Amusingly, two of the cars share the same registration number!

Rolls-Royce Silver Ghost chassis no.1907 was delivered on 16 February 1912 to Mr John M. Stephens of South Croydon. It was registered BY-1027 and bodied as a Pullman limousine by Barker & Co. of London W1. The car eventually spent many years in a private museum in south-west Scotland before being sold in 1962. It has since had several owners and is now in Ohio. The colour is metallic silver as is the Corgi model introduced in 1966 below which even shows the 'letter-box' in the windscreen – an occasional extra in the days before wipers, and also the ten-spoked front wheels and fourteen-spoked rear wheels of the Edwardian Rolls-Royce.

Addington Palace had been the country home of the Archbishops of Canterbury since 1808. In the First World War it was occupied by Canadian soldiers. Later it was the home of the Royal School of Church Music. It is located at the bottom of Gravel Hill on the A212.

To the left of the man with the goat is an Austin staff car. To the right of the goat is a Siddeley-Deasy, which could even be the car shown below it as the photographs came from the same source. When J.D. Siddeley moved from Wolseley in 1909 as manager, his cars adopted coffin-shaped bonnets and dashboard radiators (similar to Renaults). On the right is a Rover landaulette of 15 or 20 hp

This Weybridge garage building still exists. The photo *c.*1912 shows a Wolseley (left) and an Austin (right) flanking the entrance (which can be seen from within on page 96)

Below is the nicely turned-out and sign-written Panhard et Levassor a powerful chain-driven old car finding a second lease of life. A milometer is fitted to the front hub, which was readable only after dismounting.

Queen Alexandra the Queen consort of King Edward VII was born in Copenhagen and they married in 1863 when her husband was Prince of Wales. It was in 1912 that she instituted the annual Alexandra Rose Day in aid of hospitals.

Posed in Ewell High Street are a Perth (Scotland) registered Armstrong-Whitworth of 1911 on the left and a London-registered Delaunay-Belleville on the right. Both cars have their landaulette bodies open and the Armstrong-Whitworth shows it is more modern by having electric instead of oil side-lights and an AA badge with the wings that were introduced in 1911 when the AA merged with its competitor the Motor Union.

The Armstrong-Whitworth was made in Newcastle and the low snap-shut water filler cap is a feature. The Delaunay-Belleville was made near Paris by the company that had previously been well-known as locomotive and boiler-makers, hence the round bonnets and radiators. It was France's most luxurious car with a six-cylinder engine. Both cars are driven by uniformed chauffeurs, as would have been usual for owners of cars of this size and class pre-1914. Each car has one front tyre with steel studs that were supposed to be non-skid in those days. This is not braking skidding, as these are before front-wheel-brakes, but what was called 'the dreaded side slip'. The more modern Armstrong-Whitworth has detachable wheels whereas the Delaunay-Belleville has fixed wheels and rims so roadside punctures were a calamity.

This Douglas 350cc motorcycle of 1913 came from Bristol. The initials KN on the petrol tank must have been applied by the owner. More than one Brooklands racer was called KN as a joke referring to the pepper.

Two charabancs (or *chars a banc*) from c.1912. The upper one is an American Garford with pneumatic tyres on detachable rimmed wheels and presumably working out of Croydon. The lower picture shows a Manchester-built Crossley based at Epsom Downs Station and carrying a more juvenile outing.

It was common for such charabanc groups to pose for a photograph before setting out. The photographer would then hope to sell them all pictures when they returned at the end of the day.

Three ages of man! Caterham Valley Library disclosed these three photographs which one would like to think shows a happy bachelor, young family man, and the motor-car man with more responsibilities having returned from the War, except that the two wheeler is registered later than the three. Perhaps the sidecar outfit was secondhand or re-registered as it is a year or so more modern.

The motorcycle is a Premier of 1912 of 2½hp and 246cc. The logo on the tank was a kangaroo, though hopefully this did not indicate what it was like to ride! The machine is bicycle-pedal assisted for steep hills and also for starting. One got it moving by pedalling and then let in the clutch to start the motor – and this after every stop.

The combination is a Humber with basket-work chair. It dates from 1913 and is 3½hp and 500cc.

After the First World War, the Rover Co. introduced a really cheap and easy-to-run car, the Rover Eight. It was more substantial than a cycle-car but cruder than most real cars. It had a horizontally opposed air-cooled engine of 998cc. The cylinder heads stuck out either side of the bonnet behind the dummy radiator. Stories are told that cooling problems with the engine could make the heads glow red at night though these would have been invisible to the driver. The carburettor, above the engine, was gravity fed from the scuttle petrol tank whose filler can be seen on this 1921 car. Most of the lubrication was by splash, the big ends dipping into a small bath of oil as they revolved. An electric starter motor was among the optional extras at a hefty £15.

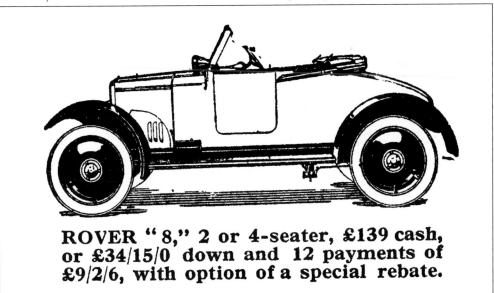

ROVER " 8," 2 or 4-seater, £139 cash, or £34/15/0 down and 12 payments of £9/2/6, with option of a special rebate.

This is the two seater with the shorter, 7ft 4in wheelbase, but the growing family found room in the dickey.

A 1912 Leyland 30hp bus awaits its passengers near the Red Cross, Reigate. Leyland Motors Ltd were at Leyland in Lancashire.

Harold Karslake astride his 1912 3½hp Rover with Armstrong hub gear 'this turned out to be a splendid machine, winning one of the Jarrott Cups and making me runner-up to George Brough in the London-Edinburgh-London Trial at Whitsun'. (Harold Karslake writing in *Veteran & Vintage Magazine* in 1956).

Finding these pictures of Sheffield-Simplex cars in the archives of the Oatlands Park Motor Co. Ltd. of Weybridge who were agents for this Sheffield-made car means they just have to be included on the assumption that these cars were actually sold from Weybridge.

Above is a tourer with body by Van den Plas and below is a two-seater with dickey seat whose step is seen above the rear wing. There is also a lower storage locker that may be designed for golf clubs.

Sheffield-Simplex had a history back to 1904 but in 1913 came the 30hp six-cylinder car, a modern-looking smooth and sophisticated car that would be enormously coveted if one re-appeared today. Starting and lighting were all electric from a flywheel-dynamotor that doubled as both dynamo and starter motor.

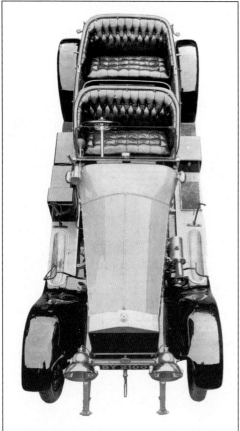

Another Rolls-Royce Silver Ghost, this time from 1913, was a torpedo tourer for Capt. Malcolm Campbell, who established World Land Speed Records eight times in the period 1924-1935 and the Water Speed Record four times. The positioning of the two spare wheels would have allowed use of the driver's door, but both the gear lever and handbrake are to the driver's right making right-hand access impractical.

The stable of Mrs Shirley Birt at Chiddingfold. On the left is a Renault two-seater of the model AX introduced for 1909. It was a two-cylinder 7/8cv of 1,060cc and good for 55kph. The model was made until 1913.

The second car (PB-2137) is a Sunbeam 12/16 tourer with a three-litre four-cylinder engine and dating from 1912. Next is another Renault. It is a very big tourer, but difficult to identify exactly as the company made a great many different models each year.

The Rolls-Royce Silver Ghost was bodied as a limousine by May & Jacobs of Guildford in 1911. The big leather box on the roof contains spare tyres.

The lower car (PA-5315) was supplied to Mr J. St. Joe Strachey of Newlands Corner, Guildford with three-quarter cabriolet body by Barker.

Cyril Patteson, Wilberforce & Co. were at the northern end of Croydon Road, Caterham Valley, c.1912/13. The premises then became The County Garage but in 1922 was bought by Fred Marden and became Layhams Engineering Co. right up until 1997 when his family sold it to the Griffin chain.

On the forecourt is a chain-driven Mercedes, possibly an older car re-bodied, an air-cooled two-cylinder Humberette and two GWKs. On the pavement is a Douglas 350cc motorcycle. The only registration readable is 'IT' which is from County Leitrim in the Irish Republic but this does not mean that the GWK ever left Surrey!

The garage advertises Shell and Pratt's petrols but no pumps are to be seen. Fuel was sold in two-gallon cans until the first pumps were installed in the twenties.

On the right is St George's Hill Golf Club, Weybridge, which was a Military Hospital in 1914 when these wounded soldiers were allowed out to play with a 1912/13 GWK.

Messrs. Grice, Weller & Keiller (the latter later being involved with marmalade from the GWK factory in Maidenhead) made cars pre-war in Datchet. The two-seater cars had two-cylinder 1,045cc rear-mounted engines driving via friction discs to chain final drive.

The GWK friction drive disc was faced with pressed paper and was pressed at right angles against the flat outside face of the flywheel. As the disc was moved further from the flywheel centre the gear ratio was gradually increased. The GWK publicity advertised it as having 'a gear for every gradient'.

77

Above and right:
Another Redhill coachbuilder was Meier & Son, established in 1864. When this Italian Itala 25hp four-cylinder rotary-valved car was made in 1913, Meier had already produced over 500 car bodies. This was their idea for a 'convertible' body which the Itala concessionaires in London offered as a new style, but the idea was not a success. The four-seater tourer could quickly be converted into a smart two-seater with big luggage rack. The back-seat back-rest folded in, the rear body sides folded across to meet in the middle and the luggage rack folded up and forward from the usual location above the petrol tank. The hood could be folded behind the rear seats or the rear part of the hood could be moved forward to the front brackets but when over the front the saddles were very close. A problem with folded hoods on veteran cars came when hitting a bump in the road. If the hood was not strapped down to the saddles it could jump up and break the hood sticks on coming down again.

This car has electric lights and an electric horn. The half-open windscreens may look odd to-day but careful angling of the glasses could make for a very much less draughty and more comfortable journey for the driver.

Two landaulettes, a Sunbeam of about 1921, 16hp, with detachable steel artillery wheels is in front of a just pre-First World War Napier 20hp. The waving waistline of the Napier indicates a British coachbuilder other than Cunard of Upper Richmond Road, Putney who built the majority of bodies for this Acton company. In 1925 Napier stopped making cars to concentrate on aeroplane engine manufacture. Moore's Presto Garage was in West Croydon and later became main agent for Morris cars.

A Douglas Ladies' Model of 1913/14 that belonged to Miss J.A. Jacobs, Superintendent of District Nurses in the Tonbridge area which may be the reason for the stork mascot. The engine was a 2¾hp (350cc) horizontal two-cylinder. These bikes had no clutch, so had to be push-started after every halt. The gentleman is William Douglas, one of the manufacturers.

To the right, and back to the 'Hut' at Wisley, a lady poses in her Bébé Peugeot, new in March 1914. This tiny car was made from 1913 to 1916. It had a T-head, four-cylinder engine of 855cc and shaft drive. The model was designed by Ettore Bugatti. The wire wheels were non-detachable so a Stepney spare wheel is carried. The extra pair of oil side-lights mounted at the front would have given much less light than the acetylenes on the scuttle and would have shaken about on their flimsy chassis mountings. However, oil lamps are more simple to light and do not leave the dirty residue that acetylene crystals entail.

BEACON CYCLECAR

Engine BEACON (made in France) 10 h.p., 85 mm. bore by 96 mm. stroke, cubic capacity 1090 c.c. Twin-cylinder V-type air-cooled engine. Zenith carburetter. Drip lubrication.

Transmission Leather cone clutch. Gate change-speed gear with three speeds and reverse giving gear ratios of 4⅛ to 1, 6¾ to 1, 10½ to 1. Transmission by shaft through gearbox to worm axle.

Wheels & Tyres Four wheels, 650 mm. by 65 mm. tyres. Wheelbase 7 ft. 6 ins., track 3 ft. 10 ins., overall length 10 ft., overall width 4 ft. 5 ins., ground clearance 8 ins.

Various Weight of chassis 6 cwt. Seating arrangements for two side by side. Rack and pinion steering. Equipment of standard machine: side and tail lamps, horn, jack, pump and tools. Price £135. Coach built or cane body.

Beacon Motors, Ltd., Liphook, Hants, and Hindhead, Surrey.

From the Beacon Hill Motor Works at Hindhead and then Liphook came the Beacon Cyclecar. The engine was a Griffon V-twin with shaft drive in 1913/14 , though JAP V-twin engines with friction drive were originally tried. The Beacon could be bought coach-built or, as here, with ultra-light canework body.

82

THE SUTTON LIMOUSINE DE LUXE.

Two from Lancia of Turin. The limousine was bodied by Harris & Others Ltd. of Clapham, for Mrs E.W. Fradgley of Viewlands, Reigate. It is on a 24/30hp chassis and probably from 1914.

If the bus is a Lanica Kappa of 4,950cc made in 1919, good for 125kph as a car, it must have been well geared down to power this coach at a maximum 'speed 12mph' The Kappa was made in 1919 with these Michelin disc wheels and this one is bodied by Warwick Motor Body Works in Croydon.

The Model 'T' Ford was in production in Detroit, US, from 1908 to 1927 and over fifteen million were made. Ford opened a factory at Trafford Park, Manchester and have made cars here ever since, moving to Dagenham in 1932. The engine was a 2.9 litre four-cylinder monobloc with detachable cylinder head. The original $850 was reduced to $260 by 1925. Its two-speed planetary gearbox was foot-pedal controlled.

These two Surrey-registered cars are 1915/16 models during the time when all Model 'T's were black. These are both Manchester-built cars with right-hand drive. Note the wartime black out of the headlamps on the upper car.

Two
Between the Wars

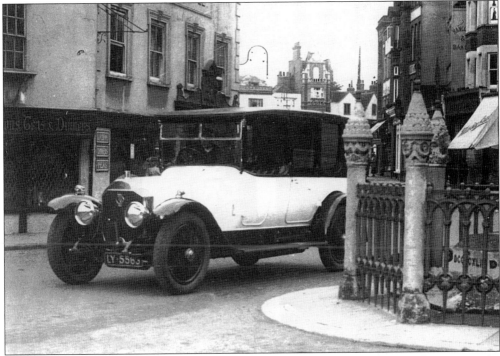

The Napier Co. at Acton had competed with Daimler, Lanchester and then Rolls-Royce at the top end of the British market. During the First World War, Napiers made aero engines eventually producing the 'Lion' W12 pattern water-cooled aero engine that was still in production through the Second World War as a marine engine.

From 1918 the company only made one car model, the 40/50 Napier and this only until 1925 when they concentrated exclusively on the aero engine side. Shown is a Napier of 1919/20 passing the Coronation Stone in Kingston, where it then stood just south of the Market Place on the junction of Thames Street, Eden Street and High Street. In the background is the tower of the Market Hall with the church tower behind it. The Coronation Stone is now sited further south in High Street outside the modern Guildhall.

How could Sturt Goatcher of Farnham have been completing a coupé body on a Studebaker made in 1915? This must be a 1919 completion. Side lights mounted ahead of the windscreen at the period were not necessary as this SD-4 model had dimmer bulbs in the headlights. By 1923, when the Studebaker below was made, sidelights were back again. In 1915, during the War, Mr McKenna became Chancellor of the Exchequer and car imports were forbidden to preserve foreign exchange and shipping space for essential goods. After the War an import duty of $33\frac{1}{3}\%$ was imposed to protect the home industry but American cars were still more than able to compete. Overland, Chrysler and Ford imported cars for assembly in Britain. In 1919 two out of every five cars on British roads were Fords from Trafford Park, Manchester. In 1925 General Motors bought Vauxhall..

This old combination with its seat not yet upholstered and suspended on 'C' springs is powered by a V-twin JAP engine of probably 1,000cc in a Chater Lea frame. It bears (BY-334) a Croydon registration of 1904/5 and yet dates from about 1920.

Of similar 1920 date is the Panther (P&M) combination below with its inclined single cylinder engine with two-speed gearbox. The turkeys are a Christmas delivery in 1925.

Under 1920s wings is a 1909 Lion Peugeot racing voiturette raced by French champion Jules Goux in 1909 and 1910. The car was acquired during the First World War by Lt Angus Maitland and brought to Hindhead where it was registered PB-565 in April 1920.

Before the War, Angus Maitland had been responsible for the Beacon light car made in Liphook and then Hindhead.

Malcolm Campbell had several houses in Surrey. His first 'Blue Bird' was basically an old Darracq in 1912. He must have bought this car in 1913. After the War, on 8 October 1920 he drove this 1912 7.6 litre Grand Prix Peugeot to take several Class G records at Brooklands. He took the flying start half-mile at 109.03 and the mile at 107.14mph. In both cases he only broke Jules Goux' record in an identical car in 1913 by less than one mile per hour. But it was well worth using as one's Christmas card surely.

The Peugeot engine was very advanced. It used four valves per cylinder (four-cylinders) inclined at forty-five degrees and operated by two overhead camshafts. The valves were operated desmodromically.

From Hersham came the ABC light car in the twenties. ABC had already made motor-cycles just before the War and the name came from 'All British (Engine) Co.' The cars of which this is a 1921 example shown outside the Hersham factory used flat-twin air-cooled front engines whose 24bhp produced a brisk performance. The ABC engine had problems on starting, lubrication and from the long pushrods to the overhead valves. The engine was also noisy. One further problem related is that the filler cap atop the false radiator (note that it was air cooled) actually led to the petrol tank! An average of less than one car per week was produced through the company's seven year life.

Registered PC-8138 in 1922 but looking older is a Chevrolet four-cylinder tourer. General Motors had taken over Chevrolet in 1917 and five years later its US sales were third behind only Ford and Dodge.

The car is parked in the centre of Shere village, outside the White Horse Inn soon after it had been 'aged' with half-timbering.

When the First World War ended in 1918 it took the motor industry some years to get back into its stride and yet the homecoming soldiers wanted transport. Some terrible motor cars were rushed into production.

Typical of these marginal cars was this Xtra made in Chertsey. It can be described as a single-seater motorcycle side-car with $3\frac{3}{4}$ hp single-cylinder engine mounted on the single back wheel. The Xtra was only made from 1922 to 1924.

Deepdene House, south-east of Dorking was built 1818-40 by Thomas Hope. From 1920 until 1939 it was an hotel and then suffered less happy times until it was demolished in 1969.

Here uniformed and medalled attendants park cars in the early twenties. Note that the majority of the cars are open-topped.

On 4 June 1923 this AEC (Associated Equipment Co. of Southall, Middlesex) K-type open-top bus was one of many loaned by the LGOC (London General Omnibus Co.) to the East Surrey Traction Co. Ltd. It was returned to the LGOC in 1930. Note the waterproof aprons for the upper-deck passengers in the upper photograph which locates the photographs as Flanchford Road on Reigate Heath, looking back towards the Black Horse public house.

Bell Street, Reigate c.1925 looking north towards the tunnel. On the left is a Standard of 11.6hp. The furthest car on the opposite kerb is an American Overland behind a delivery van. BW-3985 is an Angus Sanderson 14.3hp which was made at Hendon, Middlesex, and this one registered in Oxfordshire.

Another Standard the same as the one on the left above. Although registered in London (XT) it lived in Reigate.

Registered in Surrey in 1923 this Sentinel steam lorry is shown on contract hire in Liverpool in 1950 the year when Sentinel of Shrewsbury made their last steamers. This wagon was originally on solid tyres as is the Sentinel six-wheeler below that would have chuffed and blown smoke around Surrey in the thirties.

This lorry is probably shown before delivery as it is in front of the Sentinel Works at Shrewsbury

Left: Thames Ditton was the address of A.C. Cars Ltd. from 1922. A couple of years later the Hon. Victor Bruce was contemplating entry in the 1924 twenty-four-hour Le Mans Race and tested this Anzani-engined A.C. at Brooklands. The Members' Bridge and Test Hill are seen in the distance. The car carried a special four-seater body – in fabric to save weight – as a four-seat body was a Le Mans Race requirement. The radiator has metal rods as stoneguard and the lamps are wire stoneguarded. The car did not run at Le Mans.

In 1926 the Hon. Victor Bruce with the photographer W.J. Brunell entered a six-cylinder A.C. (below left) in the Monte Carlo Rally. He is seen at the start at John O'Groats. He was the first Briton and his A.C. the first British car to win the Monte Carlo Rally. The six-cylinder two-litre engine was used from 1922 until 1963 during which time the power output rose from 35 to 103bhp. From 1913 to 1929 the gearboxes of A.C.'s were mounted in the rear axle.

Above is a 1929/30 Magna five-seat saloon A.C. Introduced in 1928 it proved too big and too heavy to be successful and was soon dropped, though it did boast hydraulic brakes. The company was also in financial difficulty at the time. The car is seen outside 'High House', Thames Ditton, the site of A.C. Cars.

Oatlands Park Motor Co. has now become Weybridge Automobiles Ltd. and for sale in 1925 are prominently two Clynos, and a Daimler on the left and two American cars, a Chrysler and an Oldsmobile are on the right behind the Bullnose Morris.

Five years later the much improved showroom boasts (from the left) Fiat, Wolseley, Wolseley, three unclear, another Wolseley and a Riley.

Morris L-type 12cwt van *c*.1926 of Morris' own construction. The engine was an 11.9hp four-cylinder side valve and it still has brakes on the rear wheels only. One could use the step and the top of the spare tyre to access the roof rack.

This 1926 Leyland lorry on solid tyres is in the livery of the London & South Coast Transport Co. Ltd.

Knights of Reigate have been drapers from this building in Bell Street since 1883, which is now owned by fourth generation Michael Knight. This AEC charabanc was new on 7 April 1919 with body by Chalmers coachbuilders of Redhill. In 1924 it was converted to a lorry so this brackets the date of Knights' staff outing.

The Lancia Lambda of 1922 broke new ground in several ways. It was the first car in the world with 'unitary construction' principles for chassis and body. It had independent front suspension and the 2,120cc, later 2,570cc, engine was arranged as a narrow-angle 'V'.

This car dates from 1927 and is a six-light saloon. It stands outside Vigo House (which was about to be demolished) in Church Street, Weybridge.

Bell Street, Reigate, where Finch's Bicycle Shop still flourishes today. The car is a *c.*1925 Buick tourer of the new economy series called the Standard Six. The colour was Brewster green with black wings. This car has the side-lights on the wings for the British market.

The Jowett was made at Bradford. Its best period was the twenties but the horizontally opposed two-cylinder engine was used in the Jowett Bradford van through to 1953 and post-war the company came to the fore again with the Javelin and Jupiter.

This is the Jowett Long-four 7hp tourer of 1926 priced at £245. The wheels were detachable steel artilleries.Front-wheel brakes were not used until 1929.

This outing from Surrey to the seaside is in a 1927 AEC. The coach is seen again below with the hood fixed. It was one of six '419' type coaches new to Reigate Bus Garage in 1927 and used for private hire. Bus production was moved from Walthamstow to a new factory at Southall in1927, and two years later AEC introduced diesel engines.

In 1927 when this Amilcar Grand Sport left the St Denis, Paris factory it was a typical light sports car competing with Salmson. The engine was a four-cylinder side valve of 1,074cc and Amilcar's own make. The body of this car is built on the Weymann principle of fabric stretched over a wooden frame. This was lightweight and didn't rattle, but then it was not very durable.

The car was given, new, to C.W.P. Hampton for his seventeenth birthday by his father when the familly lived in Weybridge. The body was made by Boon and Porter of Castelnau, Barnes, Amilcar concessionars. In 1931 Peter Hampton past exchanged it for a Riley Nine for which Boon and Porter were then agents. The family then owned Hamptons department store in Kensington.

The Purley Council Depot in Brighton Road in 1926 houses five steamers, four lorries and a traction engine on the right. All are on solid tyres and with centre-pivot steering. Coal-fired, the lorries needed a long time each morning to fire up and have enough steam pressure to move off for their days' work. The cones and flues above the chimneys would have prevented the build-up of too much smoke in the shed.

A 1925 four-seater sports Riley RK-3997 (Croydon) rests while the map is consulted. The three sports model Rileys were known as Redwingers having polished aluminium bodies and red wings. The sports models were 10.8hp with 1,498cc engines.

A single order for nine Morris Cowley fixed-head saloons was made in 1929 by Mullard Radio Co. from the Woodcote Motor Co. Ltd. whose premises are still in Church Street, just off High Street, Epsom.

The windscreen sun-visors were standard and the 11.9hp 1,548cc had three bearings, magneto ignition and overhead camshaft.

Fixed artillery wheels with detachable rims in the twenties is often the sign of an American car. This is a 1927 or 28 Series LM Chevrolet with 25cwt van body made in Croydon by Warwick Motor Body. The cab-style seems old fashioned and front wheel brakes are still not standard.

103

The centre of Epsom on Derby Day just prior to the First World War shows congestion outside the Spread Eagle Hotel with a queue of London taxis in the foreground. Nearly twenty years later and viewed from the west a twenty horse-power Rolls-Royce with 1925 Eastbourne registration is parked on a quieter occasion. On the left appears the front of a Standard and then a Citroen and a Morris are parked.

Two views of Cheam *c.*1929 illustrate the quietness of suburbia and the variety in town.

In Malden Road, Cheam a Bullnose Morris of 1925 passes its slightly older sister. Neither car is locally registered, the parked car (DO) was registered with the County Council of Holland (later Lincolnshire) and the other car (FF) registered in Merioneth.

Below, another Morris, this time a 1929 flat-nose tourer negotiates the heavier traffic of Cheam's Broadway where a bus, horse-drawn dray, motorcycle combination, bicycles and cars are present.

The Trojan was built in Surrey. Designed by Leslie Hounsfield it was made from 1922 to 1928 by Leyland Motors in Kingston and from 1928 until the 1960s by Trojan Ltd. on Purley Way, Croydon. They were particularly to be seen puttering about in the livery of Brooke Bond Tea. Leylands made lorries, a luxury car in very small numbers in the early twenties and this elementary and cheap car. Its horizontal two-stroke, four-cylinder engine was mounted below the seats in a tray-like chassis. Its 1.5 litre engine produced only 10bhp, but these horses were developed at very low speed giving good enough power. The early cars had solid tyres which led to the story – hopefully untrue – of car wheels getting caught in tramlines.

The solid-tyred car on the left was Kingston made 1922-1925. Overleaf the Guildford milk float and the Nutfield bakery van were built at Trojan's own premises on Purley Way, Croydon whose opening is celebrated in the picture above.

Uniformed delivery drivers and a fleet of late twenties Trojan vans.

A 1929 Austin Seven but this is the semi-sports model produced by coachbuilders H. Taylor & Co. of London SW7 to sell at £165. It has fabric body, a door on the passenger side only and naval-style ventilators on the scuttle in front of the v-windscreen.

The Austin Seven was introduced in 1922 as a really small and cheap but still real motorcar. The four-cylinder engine of 747cc developed 13bhp and had brakes on all wheels. The Austin Seven was to end the era of the minimal cyclecars that had sold well to those coming home from the First War and wanting transport for the first time.

Dennis of Guildford made only fire engines and commercial vehicles from the twenties. Here 1927 and 1923 engines parade on 21 June 1929 for the funeral of J.J. Perrow, chief fire officer of Chertsey Fire Brigade from 1905 to 1929. The scene is Eastworth Road, Chertsey.

Below a 1928 Dennis fire-engine in the fleet of Caterham & Warlingham fire brigade. It looks dated being still on solid rubber tyres. The photo dates from August 1930.

Weybridge in 1928 and 1930. Wood's Garage has opened in the Holstein Hall in High Street, Weybridge. Inside is a display of La Salles (centre and centre right) and Buicks with London (MP) registrations.

The lower picture shows the outside of the Holstein Hall and a display of Vauxhalls in 1930. Left of centre is a Hurlingham two-windscreen three-seater with pointed tail, while right of centre is the Kingston coupe. Both are six-cylinder 2.9 litre T-types.

In December 1925 the British Vauxhall Motors Ltd. was bought by General Motors of America. Buick and La Salle were already makes in the General Motors Corporation.

His and Her's cars in 1929. 1929/30 was the period of the slump and Austin sales dropped nearly 10% replacing its historic annual climb. In January 1930 Sir Herbert Austin wrote 'there are two million people in Britain earning less than £7 a week who can afford to run one of the medium sized cars'. Nevertheless it was to be more than thirty years to the middle sixties before two-car families were other than a rarity.

His Austin is a 1929 16/6 Burnham saloon with added opera lights. Madame has bought the new six-cylinder Morris Oxford sliding roof coupe. Heaters in cars were not standard until the sixties so they have given each other fur gauntlets for Christmas! Both cars are Croydon registered.

Edward Abbott of Farnham took over the business of Page and Hunt in 1929 to create E.D. Abbott Ltd, coachbuilders. These two Austin Sevens would have been among his first products, dating from early (PG) and late (PL) 1930. Both were built on the principles created and patented by Charles Weymann. In the French Air Force during the First World War Weymann created a technique to build flexible and lightweight car bodies. The wooden frame members did not touch but had steel plates as joining-pieces to avoid creaking noises. American cloth was stretched over the frame, panelled and padded where appropriate. This has allowed the above-the-waist material colour to be different and match the wing colour of the upper car whilst the lower car has 'driver's helmet' wings and no running boards.

Two St John Ambulances pose in Massetts Road, Horley close to Branch Brothers butcher's shop. The front vehicle is a 1929 Chevrolet two-stretcher ambulance featuring a fabric body. It was on the LQ 1½ ton chassis. The tall body had interior lights and frosted glass side windows with ventilators above. The Croydon (VB) registration is early 1930. Behind is a 1927 Morris Commercial T-type Tonner originally registered with Leicester County Council (UT).

The lower Chevrolet 1½ ton lorry dates from 1930 when it must be shown doing its demonstration climb of Box Hill. Hanging behind it is an enormous wooden wheel chock.

This garage in South Street, Dorking of F.W. Mays is now a Rover showroom but in 1930 it held an agency for Citroen and three C6 Citroen saloons are displayed outside. The engine was a six-cylinder of 2,442cc and surprisingly all these cars have wire-spoked wheels instead of the solid disc Michelin wheels of the standard Citroens in their native France.

In 1930 the Armstrong Siddeley Twelve two-seater still had its sphinx mascot sitting up (compare with the 1933 Armstrong Siddeley on page 119). Always a quality car, this 12hp six-cylinder was the base model at £250 for the two-seater. Capacity was 1,434cc but side valves and a three-speed box did not make it a performer.

This doesn't immediately look like a Standard but it is an Envoy Light Six which was top of the range in 1931 and this one has two-colour paint and wheel discs. Some cars with doors opening apart had no central pillar but this is not one.

Above and two years later is this Standard Little Nine saloon with sliding roof. Standard's cheapest offering at £155 with 1,006cc engine. It has a Croydon registration.

1932 Reigate Borough Carnival.

Looking north up London Road, Reigate outside the old Wray Park Garage where a Lanchester awaits a buyer under a sign saying Humber. The level crossing is just out of sight in the background. Only the building behind the broken car still exists today.

What a wonderful sight for modern old-car enthusiasts to see a Delage with twin side-mounted spare wheels that could only have been about five years old in 1932 already converted to breakdown duties.

The notice on the car behind reads 'This error of judgement cost over £450. Let your mottoe be Safety First. Four lives were endangered'. Notice that the car had a plate-glass windscreen.

Below is the inside of the Wray Park Garage in London Road, Reigate. The balcony in the background is at the back of the front showroom above. These must be secondhand cars as they are of various dates but nearly all are 1930s Morrises.

In 1934 Chrysler of America introduced a radically new design of car. Its shorter bonnet and longer body shell were too much for most buyers and Chrysler's more conventional cars sold much better. The De Soto and Plymouth names were launched in 1928 to be slightly cheaper cars. This car is about to be driven by Miss Burtenshaw in West Street, Reigate. This De Soto SE four-door sedan was sold in England as the Chrysler Croydon.

The new streamlined Airflows of 1934 had built-in headlamps, three-abreast seating, radiator well forward of the front axle, unitary construction and four-wheel hydraulic brakes.

A Leyland Tiger coach, bodied by Burtenshaws of Reigate.

APL114 is a 1934 registration for this O.M. and so not only after O.M. had been bought by Fiat but also several years after the company appears to have made it's last car. This must be one of the cars assembled by the British concessionaires. A 2.2 litre six-cylinder engine powered these sporting Italian cars and this one is doing a driving test in a Welsh Rally.

An Armstrong Siddeley of 1933. It is a 15hp saloon with six-cylinder engine of 1,930cc and 'special incorporated four-speed self-changing gear' which today we would call a pre-selector gearbox.

In 1919 the firm of Armstrong-Whitworth based in Newcastle amalgamated with Siddeley-Deasy of Coventry (see 1913 example in this book). Armstrong Siddeley were to make good quality family cars until the Sapphire range ceased in 1960.

A 1934 S.S.II saloon is parked outside the church in Ewhurst. The model was to evolve into the S.S. Jaguar 100. During the War the letters S.S. became associated with undesireable images so the company changed its name to that of its top pre-war model, 'Jaguar'.

The Series I Morris 5cwt van of 1934. This was a Morris Eight, the car that headed Morris Motors Ltd through the depression years. In 1935 Road Fund Tax was reduced from £8 to £6 per annum. To keep the price down to compete with the £100 Ford saloon the Morris Series I was sold without trafficators or bumpers.

John Cobb specialised in big cars at Brooklands Track and attacks on the Land Speed Record, which he took in 1938 at 350.20mph at Bonneville in the US. Above he returns to the Brooklands Paddock in the Napier-Railton after setting a new Brooklands lap record at 139.71mph (224.79kph) on 2 April 1934.

Below, John Cobb makes a pit-stop in the BRDC 500 at Brooklands on 21st September 1935. Dunlop Mac fits a wheel while Fiddle Hick approaches with the wheelnut hammer. Ken Taylor adjusts Cobb's seat.

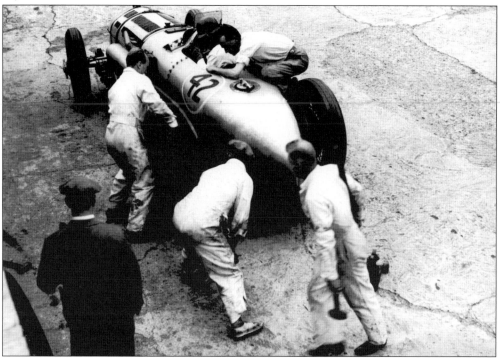

The centre of Reigate in 1933 when the High Street was still two-way and the directions north are through the tunnel. An open-top AEC bus of 1926 takes on passengers while four Daimler(?) limousines wait as taxis opposite.

A 1936 Hillman '80' limousine. At this time Hillman offered four sizes of chassis and a total of ten different body styles from the Minx saloon (shown on page 7) at £159 to this one, above, at £395. New for 1936 was the adoption of independent front wheel suspension that the company called 'Evenkeel'. The six-cylinder side-valve engine was rated at 20.8hp from its 3,181cc. The central spotlight and the two external horns are extras.

Top of the Vauxhall range in 1936 was this Big Six Regent limousine. The car used the Bedford 3.2 litre engine and the body was designed by Grosvenor.

The original No.1 HRG. It was made at Hampden Road, Norbiton in early 1936. Production cars were made at Oakcroft Road, Tolworth and the company made traditional sports cars in the style set by Frazer Nash until 1956. For its first years, 1924-1926 Frazer Nash was also a Surrey car made in London Road, Kingston.

The HRG two-seater used a 1½ litre Meadows 4ED engine, Moss gearbox, ENV rear axle and some other bought-out parts. Later cars used Singer engines.

This HRG is being used by Guy Robins (the R of HRG) to climb Darracott on the 1936 London to Lands End Trial.

Stoneman Funeral Directors, of Redhill, who in 1999 updated their fleet to new Daimlers bought these three Rolls-Royces in 1937. They are posed outside Brockham church. The lead car is an early Phantom I so at least ten years old when entering the funeral trade whereas the other two cars

A Surrey registered (GPB 2) car in the Surrey setting of Friday Street, south-west of Dorking. The car is a Bugatti Type 57S of 1937. This is the Atalante coupe one of Jean Bugatti's designs with a very raked windscreen for its time.

The car was on the Bugatti stand at the London Motor Show in 1938. The purchaser already owned two other Bugatti's and all his cars were painted white with black roof and wings. Since the war the car was for many years owned by the president of the Bugatti Club of America.

are later Phantom I models so could date from 1929. The bodies are all by Dottridge. The second and third cars were called convertible hearses in that they could be used as a full hearse, a child hearse or a full limousine. After the War they were part-exchanged for a fleet of Austin Princesses.

Early in 1935 the Rootes Group took over Sunbeam-Talbot-Darracq and the next year Rootes brought out an up-market Hillman Minx called the Talbot Ten as 'Britain's Most Exclusive Light Car'. This one dates from 1938 and is a pretty drop-head with body by E.D. Abbott of Farnham.

Sir Malcolm favours Hercules Safety Models

𝒮ir Malcolm Campbell is, of course, famous as the holder of the World's Land Speed Record at 301·128 m.p.h. and is probably the most brilliant and successful racing driver of the age. It is less generally known that he is also a keen and practical cyclist. We are, therefore, proud that Sir Malcolm has chosen Hercules Safety Models, not only for himself, but for Lady Campbell and their two children, and we take this opportunity to express our gratitude to him for allowing us to use the photograph above.

Sir Malcolm Campbell had several Surrey homes but this photo is probably from his period at Roundwood, Povey Cross. The white shed where his record cars were prepared is still behind the lodge where his mechanic Leo Villa lived.

Campbell broke the World's Land Speed Record at Bonneville, Utah on 3rd September 1935 and was knighted.

On the left is Donald Campbell who raised the Land Speed Record to 403.1 at Lake Eyre, Australia in 1964. He took the World's Water Speed Record seven times between 1955 and 1964 and was killed on 4 January 1967 at Lake Coniston while attempting to raise it again.

The same but different are these two cars assembled at Mortlake Road, Kew. Both come from the Chrysler Corporation and both are basically Plymouths except that the Plymouth name was not used in England. Above is the Dodge Six of 1937 but Dodge only supplied the grille and corporate identity items. In 1937 Dodge was America's fourth largest car maker.

Below is the Chrysler Kew Six of 1938 which again uses Plymouth body and mechanicals. The cars were shipped from Chrysler in Canada and new to the model were hidden horn trumpets, 'no-draft' ventilation, all-steel disc wheels, hydraulic brakes and a new hypoid rear axle allowing a flat rear floor.

Farewell to Surrey with a Thames Ditton car a 16/80 A.C. pictured in August 1939, a peaceful motoring scene just before war started again.

Acknowledgements

What has made the search, research and assembly of these pictures such a pleasure has been the contact with like-minded friends. Outside my own collection I have received pictures and, more importantly, encouragement from:

Peter Brockes
Bryan Davies
Tim Harding
Malcolm Jeal
Eric Parsons

Desmond Peacock
Jane Pedler
Nic Portway
Eric Rawlinson
Brian Reynolds
A.D. Rubie (via Tim Harding)
John Stoneman

Other pictures, information and/or assistance came from:-

Sutton Archive & Local Studies Collection
John Tarring
Philip Toler

M Burtenshaw
Caterham Valley Library
Chertsey Museum
Tom Clarke
Ian Dussek
Richard Eastmead
Elmbridge Museum
Ewell Library
David Hales
The Museum of Farnham
Christopher Finch
Ian Fuller
Bob Freeman and Dick Birkhead
Horley Local History Society
Michael Knight
Geoffrey Morris
John Morris

The Veteran Car Club of Great Britain
Christopher Western
Don Williams
David Woodburn

Thanks also for the encouragement from:-

Peter Daniels
David Fitton
David Hales
Clive Willoughby
Michael Worthington-Williams

Finally, I wish to thank my wife, Mary, for her encouragement and our friend Jacqueline Bennett who has transcribed it all.